Tate -

Since the day that
your Mom and Dad told us
that you were going to be our
grandson my heart has been filled
with love and happiness! You are
bringing so much excitement and fun into
our lifes! And I will treasure every day
that we can be together!

Love - Grandma

Christmas - 2020

BEFORE YOU WERE OURS

Written by Didi Cooper

Illustrated by Holly Ross

For my grandson, Landon
Our sun, our stars, our moon

———— ⋆ ★ ⋆ ————

Before you were ours…

You were the bright stars
twinkling in the night sky
And enchanted moonbeams
shining upon the earth

Before you were ours…

You were the warm sun
   spreading kindness and love
And colorful flowers singing
   beautiful songs in the meadow

Before you were ours…

You were the gentle breeze
  giggling on a warm spring day
And fluffy clouds playfully rollicking
  far above the ground

Before you were ours…

You were the cleansing rain
   strumming a perfect tune
And the falling snow
   laying a soft blanket upon the ground

So...

We wished upon the stars and the moon
And asked the sun and the flowers

We shouted into the silly breezes
And raised our arms to the clouds above

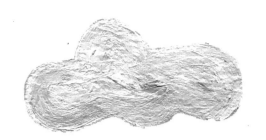

We danced in the rain
   and made angels in the snow
And hoped with all the love in our hearts
   that the time to meet you was near

And then, with all the magic
    of the stars and the moon
And all the love of the sun and the flowers

And with all the power of the
   breezes and the clouds
And the blessings of the rain and the snow

It happened.

On the most perfect day
You were ours and we were yours

Now…

Look to the stars and the moon,
  the sun and the flowers
The breezes and the clouds,
  the rain and the snow

And…

Carefully watch them twinkle,
    shine, sing, dance, and celebrate
The most beautiful, magical,
    and incredible day you became ours.

ABOUT THE AUTHOR

Didi Cooper holds a doctorate in Educational Leadership from Southern Connecticut State University and has been a career educator and an accomplished school leader. Didi recently moved to Kennebunkport, Maine, with her husband and three tiny dogs to live her best and most authentic life. *BEFORE YOU WERE OURS* was inspired by her first, and most perfect grandchild, Landon. Didi Cooper is a pen name.

ABOUT THE ILLUSTRATOR

Holly Ross graduated from the Rhode Island School of Design and has been living and creating art in Kennebunkport, Maine, for 25 years. Her whimsical designs can be spotted up and down the coast of Maine. She loves nothing more than making a beautiful mess and living with paint in her hair.